NAOMI LEFF
INTERIOR DESIGN

Kimberly Williams
Foreword by Paige Rense

The Monacelli Press

The publisher would like to thank the Pratt Institute
Library and the Naomi Leff estate for their permission
to include images in this book.

First published in
the United States of America
in 2008 by
The Monacelli Press,
a division of Random House, Inc.
1745 Broadway
New York, New York 10019

Library of Congress
Cataloging-in-Publication Data
Williams, Kimberly (Kimberly Carole)
Naomi Leff: interior design / Kimberly Williams;
foreword by Paige Rense.
        p.   cm.
ISBN 978-1-58093-200-4
1. Leff, Naomi, 1938–2005—Themes, motives. 2. Interior
decoration—United States—History—20th century. I. Title.
NK2004.3.L44W55   2008
747.092—dc22   2008000837

Printed and bound in Italy

Designed by Michelle Leong

CONTENTS

FOREWORD

We refer to "career-making moments" as those early instances in which hard work and good fortune collide, resulting in an explosion of public attention that leaves an indelible mark and sets someone on his or her way. For interior designers, those moments typically come in the form of once-in-a-lifetime commissions—often for high-profile clients—that capture the public imagination and turn the designers, for a while at least, into celebrities. Most of these designers do not expect to land these kinds of commissions over and over again. They know they're lucky to have landed even one—the one that earned them entry into an exclusive club.

Naomi Leff was one of the rare designers who shot to the top of the A list and simply stayed there. Every one of her commissions was of the sort that would have completely changed the life of almost any other interior designer; for Naomi, though, the spectacular was routine. Her star turn came when she turned New York's Rhinelander Mansion into Ralph Lauren's flagship store, in the process inventing a new kind of retail environment that would immediately become a standard. A career-making moment, certainly: but then, miraculously, she went on to experience one of these moments after another, somehow creating an entire career out of high points: homes for Tom Cruise and Nicole Kidman, Steven Spielberg, David Geffen, Mike Nichols and Diane Sawyer; retail spaces for

Armani, Gucci, and Ferragamo; private planes and yachts for some of the biggest bold-faced names in business, Hollywood, and media.

Whenever she would appear in *Architectural Digest*, which was often, we'd be flooded with letters testifying to her genius for scale, selection, elegance, and color. For one issue we had the difficult task of narrowing the list of the world's best designers to a scant thirty "deans of design"; there was simply no question that Naomi would be on it. By that point, she had grown into a contemporary legend, the designer that every movie star or media mogul simply had to—*had to*—have for their next project, or that every upscale clothier was demanding for their newest store. And it wasn't simply a matter of heat. So-called hot designers come and go, often burning out as quickly as they come to light. But Naomi's clients saw what we at the magazine saw, and what our readers saw: that she was truly great, destined for the history books as one of the very best, and that anyone would be foolish not to avail themselves of her immense talents while they had the opportunity. That opportunity no longer exists, and it makes me and countless others very, very sad. But how wonderful that we all kept her so busy, and that she in return gave us so many incredible spaces to enjoy.

Paige Rense

INTRODUCTION

Naomi Leff, one of the leading figures of interior design in the United States, came to her profession with an extraordinary gift for creative thought. At once an interpreter of historic genres of decoration and a creator of contemporary works of great theatricality, she produced interiors of timeless elegance and lucid serenity. Leff had an innate appreciation and respect for all things aesthetic, and her work was straightforward, clear, and free from excess ornamentation. Her sophisticated, simple forms demanded elegant, rich materials. She was a pioneer who challenged established methods and developed new levels of interpretation, and she was a perfectionist, stopping at nothing to see that her interiors were realized exactly as imagined.

Leff's projects were easily recognizable, yet she was known for not limiting herself to one particular style. She once said, "Anything can look beautiful: it's all about how you put it together." While she favored the fine French decorative arts of the 1920s and 1930s, she was equally drawn to the bold and graphic forms of Western and Native American traditions. Leff moved among such models with facility, fashioning a remarkably diverse range of designs: a grand New York mansion for Polo Ralph Lauren, a colonial retreat for a vacation community in Florida, an Art Deco townhouse in New York, a Western fantasy for a Colorado conference center, a serene showcase for Giorgio Armani. Each singular work assembled architectural composition, scenographic lighting, scrupu-lously conceived and executed furniture designs, painstakingly selected decorative objects, and often, important works of art.

She was known for a fanatical focus on her clients' wishes. Drawing on her background in commercial design, Leff created backdrops to highlight her patrons' preferred styles of art, furniture, and fashion. Her ideal was to modernize the traditional, concentrating on balance, scale, shape, and texture and giving pride of place to those objects cherished by a client. She accentuated the good while editing the not so good, however diverse the scheme.

Apparent in all facets of Leff's life was a compulsion to find the root solution. Never opting for the easiest answer, she studied and researched each problem, whether it would result in a five-dollar or a five-million-dollar resolution. She applied the same technique to everything she set out to do: learning to drive, to ski, to ride horses. She took up every challenge, design or otherwise, with characteristic commitment.

Early Life and Education

Naomi Leff was born in the Parkchester area of the Bronx on August 5, 1938. Her father, Frank Leff, worked for the American Jewish Committee, and her mother, Johanna, was a schoolteacher. Naomi was an imaginative child, with a delicate complexion, flaming red hair, and brilliant blue eyes. She attended the High School of Music and Art in New York City and then the State University of New York at Cortland; she graduated in 1960 with a bachelor's degree in education and sociology.

Dr. Rozanne Brooks, a professor in the sociology/anthropology department at SUNY, would remain a mentor throughout Leff's life. In addition to writing and lecturing about the role of women in society, Brooks was interested in fashion's relationship to social change, traveling and studying native dress across the globe. During her travels, Brooks purchased ethnographic objects from their makers or owners. Leff, too, studied the role of women in society. Like Brooks, she traveled to places to study native lifestyle and dress, although Leff's similar interests would play out in different ways.

After SUNY Leff studied in the master's program in sociology at the University of Wisconsin. With her newly acquired degree, and encouraged by her parents, she took up a teaching post at Primary School 41, an experimental elementary school in Manhattan. A close childhood friend, Bill Morrill, was a fellow teacher and confidant who nicknamed her "Red." The two often met to discuss liberal politics and humanistic values. Morrill remembers Leff's decision to study interior design, something that would inspire her own passions—instead of dutifully meeting her parents' expectations—using a small inheritance from her mother. In 1966, she began classes at the New York School of Interior Design, and in 1973, at the age of thirty-four, she

earned a master's degree with honors in environmental and interior design from the Pratt Institute School of Architecture.

For her master's thesis, Leff proposed a renovation of the U.S. Custom House in New York City. Designed in 1907 by Cass Gilbert in late French Renaissance style, this extraordinary building is situated in the heart of New York's financial district. But by 1973, it was vacant and unused. For Leff, the building encapsulated all elements of a "public office" of power and importance, and she was captivated by the nobility and scale of its architectural form.

Leff's project restored the historic elements of the building while transforming it into a center for the civic life of the city around Wall Street—a venue for the financial community to meet and exchange ideas. In addition, her research and analysis revealed that within ten years Battery Park City and Manhattan Landing would see a huge surge in residential population and that lower Manhattan would need to meet the demands of full-time residents. Accordingly, she planned the Custom House to serve as a social venue for these inhabitants as well. She wrote:

The proximity of [existing business] organizations would permit the pooling of their resources for general facilities such as library and research, large and small meeting halls, exhibit spaces and res-

taurants. These general facilities would also serve the residential population as a downtown cultural center. The large meeting halls would become a performing hall. The library would be a branch of the New York Library at a time when there is no branch in the area, with it specializing in business and commerce. Exhibit space containing subject matter related to the business world would be designed for the public with forums and seminars being conducted here.

Her thesis received enthusiastic and favorable responses from those in public office. James Parton, director of planning study at the nonprofit Custom House Institute and former president of the American Heritage Publishing Company, wrote to Leff on December 7, 1973:

Many of the ideas you set forth in your thesis are now under serious consideration, such as, theater and exhibition space, an orientation center, use of the rotunda area as a public space, a chamber orchestra hall and, of course, the above mentioned Public Library installation . . . Because of the direct relevance of your research, I am taking the liberty of forwarding your thesis to . . . I. M. Pei [& Partners, architectural consultants for the Custom House].

Leff also received a favorable reaction from Julia Brody of the New York Public Library. The building would remain largely empty until the 1990s, when Ehrenkrantz Eckstut and Kuhn Architects sympathetically restored it. It is interesting that the vision

expressed by Leff as a student in 1973—demonstrating her rare combination of skill, foresight, and pragmatic use of her academic background—hewed so closely to what was ultimately realized some twenty years later.

After graduating from Pratt, Leff was hired by the architectural firm John Carl Warnecke & Associates. Her work there, for interior designer Eleanor Le Maire, included retail projects for Bergdorf Goodman in White Plains, New York (featured in 1975 editions of both *Architectural Record* and *Interior Design*), and Neiman Marcus in Chicago. Upon her departure, the firm noted, "Naomi Leff has made a valuable contribution to our practice through her particular awareness of the socio-environmental aspects of interior design."

In 1975, after leaving Warnecke & Associates, Leff spent five years as a designer at Upper East Side department store Bloomingdale's. At the time, Bloomingdale's, under pioneering store designer Barbara D'Arcy and her philosophy of ever-changing store configurations, represented the cutting edge of retail. Leff was constantly challenged to design new layouts, lighting, and merchandise displays. It was also during this time that she grew confident enough in her abilities to launch a career as an independent designer.

Naomi Leff & Associates
Leff launched her own design company in 1980, at

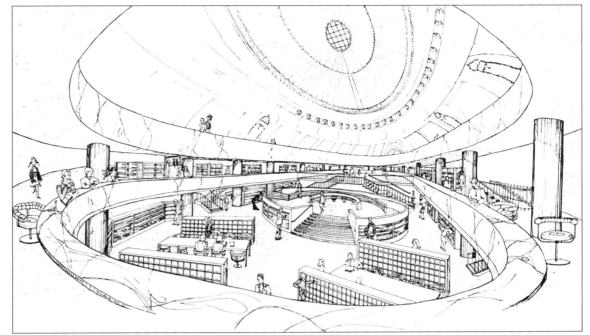

the age of forty-two. She briefly shared offices with colleagues on East Twenty-sixth Street off Madison Square Park. Women-owned businesses in the United States were on the rise in this era, but so were their failures. Leff was undaunted. Her work had become a mark of distinction; at Bloomingdale's, business in the men's shoe department tripled after her redesign. The early years were a struggle, and Leff had to content herself with a series of less significant jobs. Her first career-making moment came about in 1982, when Ralph Lauren walked into her professional life. He was planning to launch a revolutionary design concept: Ralph Lauren Home. Nancy Vignola, then vice president of home design, and Buffy Birrittella, then vice president of advertising and communications and currently executive vice president of women's design and advertising, were leading the search for an interior designer. In addition to interviewing many prominent figures, they took the time to meet Naomi Leff, an unknown name in the industry. In a manner that came to be her signature approach, Leff prepared scrupulously for the presentation of her concept, and this undiscovered designer was then commissioned to create a showroom consisting of realistic tableaus showing off the collection. As Leff recalled in an interview with Lauren's biographer, Colin McDowell,

The night before the showroom was to be presented to Ralph I was working so hard I had no sleep, so in the morning, I went home to shower and change. When I arrived, Ralph, Ricky and the

kids were there and they had already moved to the second room. I walked in and there were tears in his eyes. It was very emotional for him because it wasn't just a showroom. He was seeing a new business born. So, of course, I got emotional too, especially when he said, "How do you know about quality?" It was such a question. I remember after the presentation he said, "Why are you sad? I sense that you are sad." In that marvelous voice of his. I could hardly speak but I managed to say, "Well, for me it's an end but for you it's a beginning." To my utter amazement he replied, "Oh, no. I have lots of work for you."

Lauren was as good as his word. In numerous projects for the fashion designer, Leff built a reputation for quality and laid the foundation for the next phase of her career. Leff and Lauren teamed to design Polo stores in New York City, Beverly Hills, Philadelphia, Manhasset, Greenwich, and Birmingham, Michigan; international stores in Paris, Deauville, Munich, Montreal, and Tokyo; and his own family retreat, the Double RL Ranch, in Colorado. It was the New York Polo store, designed in 1986 in the historic Rhinelander Mansion on Madison Avenue, more than any other project that propelled her into the highest echelon of interior designers. Lauren wanted a setting unique to his mens- and womenswear, a novel concept at the time. Leff restored to the twenty-five-thousand-square-foot mansion its turn-of-the-century elegance and classicism. Though there was little left of the original interior appointments, Leff painstakingly

produced Lauren's vision. As a result, exciting, glamorous, interesting commissions poured in, such as the flagship store for Holt Renfrew in Canada for clients Hilary and W. Galen Weston.

Leff met Giorgio Armani when she designed the Armani boutique in the Holt Renfrew store. The Italian designer then commissioned her to design stores bearing the Armani name in Boston, Chicago, Palm Beach, and San Francisco. Most important, several years later he asked her to develop and design a brand image for A/X Armani Exchange. The concept was born from Armani's idea to start a jeans business for the young generation. Defining the business was a long and arduous process, for Armani and Leff both. Leff listened intently to Armani's ideas and simultaneously researched him and his work in depth, gathering every article ever written about him.

In the concept boards Leff presented for A/X, she built on the essential idea, which was to merchandise jeans. Armani's favorite piece of architecture was the steel and glass Maison de Verre, designed by Pierre Chareau in Paris in 1931. Leff introduced images of this residence into her story boards along with the Quonset hut Chareau built in East Hampton, New York, in 1946 for abstract expressionist painter Robert Motherwell. Armani responded immediately to Leff's presentation, particularly her efforts to learn about him. A/X Armani Exchange in Soho, completed in 1992, won Leff first prize at

ARMANI JEANS / SIMINT

the Institute of Store Planners Awards and was the first in a series of A/X stores worldwide.

One of Leff's joys in working with Giorgio Armani was a shared sense of pleasure in the subtleties of color. She considered it a privilege to work with people who were masters in their own right, from internationally acclaimed fashion designers to specially trained artisans, and with Armani, she took the opportunity to learn all she could about color. After Leff designed the interior of Steven Spielberg's guest house in East Hampton, the filmmaker told *Architectural Digest*, "Naomi has one of the best color senses of anyone I've met . . . She'd make a great cinematographer."

A Modern Style
Many of Leff's clients were film stars, filmmakers, and powerful executives, people with strong opinions and discerning taste. They wanted only Leff to create their homes, offices, airplanes, and yachts; she, in turn, was devoted to her patrons. Leff saw these glamorous projects as backdrops for unique and extraordinary lives. The very nature of these commissions, with generous budgets that allowed her to pursue a perfection that may have been unattainable on more typical projects, granted Leff freedom as a designer.

She produced rooms, furniture, and fixtures of a scale and design that was tailored and elegant; all the while, form would follow function. Leff applied

these guidelines while taking into account the personal style and preferences of the client. She didn't see the need to have a signature style—it was not an important point. Rather, she met the challenge of moving from style to style not only with great pleasure but with great ease, and she relished the opportunity for in-depth study of each particular genre. When Leff was inducted into the *Interior Design* magazine Hall of Fame, she said, "Being a designer means listening to your clients, seeing their vision and then interpreting."

Leff began each project by focusing on its location and surroundings. She might reflect the environment of a city apartment, for instance, with bold woods and metals. Luxurious textures—velvet, suede, and chenille—made for a cosseting atmosphere away from the strains of city life. In a beachside house, she would use more subtle materials; muted paint tones, often glazed; and lighter timbers accented by darker woods or metal. Fabrics would be relaxed linens and cottons. Leff's color palette was specific to each client, referring to an artwork, perhaps, or to the natural surroundings. A linking hue in paint colors, wood tones, metals, fabrics, furnishings, and accessories created a sense of continuity.

A feeling for traditional refinement is apparent in Leff's use of luxurious materials: leathers in all variations, specialty woods, skins, lacquer, metal, stone, and hand-woven fabrics. She used them in an understated fashion, allowing them to be

admired for their innate qualities. Leff had the ability to imbue a purely functional item with physical beauty by placing it in a context where it could be admired or by having it made to her own design in a plush material.

She emphasized the quality of craftsmanship as well as materials and their application. One of Leff's favored materials was shagreen, a coarsely textured stingray skin with enamel-like hardness and sheen. In the eighteenth century, French artisan Jean-Claude Galuchat fashioned shagreen into various artifacts for Louis XV. The material was revived in the 1920s when it became widely used by Art Deco designers. For the foyer of a client's apartment in New York's Pierre Hotel, Leff designed a shagreen console with a compound curve. According to craftsman Jean-Paul Viollet, "Making it was an almost miraculous tour de force." Each step in the process presented new and unforeseen technical trials and demonstrated the level of quality that Leff demanded.

She could not place a high enough importance on lighting and its role in conveying mood and atmosphere. Leff spent countless hours, in almost every case in collaboration with lighting designer Craig Roberts, designing, concealing, and manipulating each and every setting to illuminate those elements she wanted to focus on. The precise placement of each accessory was equally significant. Leff situated the objects as if they were on display in a gallery.

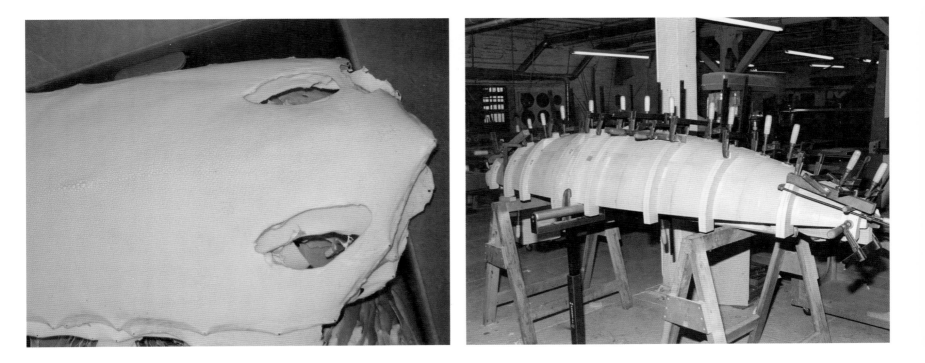

Although Leff respected design of every era and culture, she was known early in her career for an attraction to the Western and Native American aesthetic, first fostered by her projects for Ralph Lauren. The natural splendor of the American West was new to the New York–born and –raised Leff. On her travels in the western United States, Leff found the indigenous architecture and art extremely appealing. She considered it graphic, bold, and dynamic—truly modern. It was a learning experience for her, one she embraced wholeheartedly. Leff attended Indian Week, Santa Fe's annual antique ethnographic art show, coming to know the community. She draped herself in Native American jewelry when she visited, just as the locals did, wearing stacks of necklaces, belts, bracelets, and rings she acquired through the years, and she insisted that anyone accompanying her do the same.

The influence of Native American culture is evident in Leff's work. She became a collector of Indian artifacts, incorporating them as design motifs and accessories in diverse and disparate schemes. The colors, shapes, and geometric patterns are a thread, sometimes almost indiscernible, within her projects and chart the progress of her creative thinking.

Along with her exceptional interpretations of Native American and Western traditions, Leff was perhaps most enthralled by the *style moderne* and Art Deco. These early-twentieth-century movements had their roots in the middle and end of the nine-

teenth century, a period that witnessed a conscious fusion of decorative refinement and functional purpose. The 1925 Paris Exposition Internationale des Arts Décoratifs et Industriels Modernes, which saw the birth of the term "art deco," gave full expression to the new breed of architects and furniture and interior designers. The creators of Art Deco fall into three general categories: modernists, traditionalists, and individualists. Modernists, such as the architects Le Corbusier and Pierre Chareau, set out to produce expressive yet functional designs. They believed that form should follow function and sought perfection in the efficiency and effectiveness of a design. Traditionalists, such as Emile-Jacques Ruhlmann, followed similar fundamental principles but made use of sumptuous and unusual finishes: complex marquetry in rare woods, inset panels of expensive hides, and inlay made of ivory and mother of pearl. Considering themselves the heirs of eighteenth- and early-nineteenth-century cabinetmakers, they created formal, elegant, and pure forms in rich, luxurious materials. Individualists, such as Eileen Gray, drew from both strains of the Art Deco. They used more avant-garde materials and allowed diverse influences—African or Japanese forms or cubism, for instance—into their work.

Leff's own desire to strike a balance between principles laid down by traditionalists and modernists fueled her attraction to the Art Deco movement.

Her affinity with Art Deco went deeper than a passion for its style, however. Its complex evolution from amorphous shapes and influences into a highly controlled and disciplined art form mirrors much in Leff's own development as a designer. This was a movement that was sophisticated and fun, explosive and innovative, daring and exotic. The elements that define Art Deco seem to define Naomi Leff as well.

A Woman of Design

Between 1980 and 2005, Naomi Leff navigated her namesake firm from one remarkable project to another. Her vigor knew no limits; she was capable of working anywhere in the world, at all hours, without fail, seven days a week. Leff was a complex individual, a powerful woman with impeccable character, spectacular taste, and high standards. "She was an artist, a unique spirit who heard a different sound," remembers client and friend Margaret Sharkey.

In appearance and demeanor Leff was impressive and grand. She was at all times clad in black and accessorized with pieces from her collection of Art Deco jewelry. Her mischievous smile and indelible humor were treasured by everyone she knew, although she sacrificed a personal life for her professional achievements. Cautious and concentrated, Leff forged her own path yet managed to retain a certain humility given her outstanding accomplishments.

No matter how big or small, she gave equal importance to every aspect of her design—the geometry and scale of an architectural element; the precision in the application of each material; the relevance, color, shape, and placement of an accessory. A tough taskmaster who liked to be in charge, Leff took pride in applauding her clients' or a member of her own design team's contribution to a project. She felt it was her duty to educate her associates and pass on her knowledge, and she took pride in the growth and development of her office. She was known to dispatch team members to, for instance, an exotic wood specialist to learn specific methods of cutting and slicing timber to produce various types of veneer.

Filing drawers throughout Leff's office, by then located on Twenty-seventh Street in Manhattan, contained thousands of systematically organized images from international design and fashion publications. An independent library contained design publications, as well as fabric samples in an enormous variety of colors, weaves, textures, and costs. In addition, the office housed an archive of woods, skins, stone, and metal, including mockups of all the architectural details she had designed. With each new project, additional samples and materials were added to her collection.

Leff used her image archive to create concept, or storytelling, boards for each project. Once she understood the client's vision, she would pull from her files illustrations that demonstrated the desired color, form, or mood. For example, if a client's preference ran to wood paneling in the color of a golden retriever, Leff would gather all available depictions of golden retrievers and select one for the boards. The rigorously edited conceptual images illustrated only the clearest of her intentions, and she would act out the boards for her clients. "When she was presenting or talking to a client, it was really a performance," remembers former Leff associate Eva Frank. "She was acting, and she relied on me to be her eyes and ears, to listen and take notes while she focused on how she was doing." The feedback extracted from her clients was essential in refining the direction of the project.

Equally essential was the brief period of time before the completion of each project, particularly residential projects. Leff would ask the clients to stay away from the site for three weeks. She would spend the first week arranging the furniture and objects. The second week, in her office, was dedicated to honing and fine-tuning the furniture. Cushions were sent back on virtually every occasion. The staff at Naomi Leff & Associates combed the world for items the designer thought were conspicuous by their absence. Leff always fixated on at least one item. For the HR Helena Rubinstein Beauty Gallery & Spa, it was the degree of opacity in the glass. On a project for a yacht, it was the ship's wheel and chairs for the exterior decks. There was always something.

Leff spent the third week on her final decoration, known as the "Naomi touch." She carried out last-minute adjustments and almost imperceptible changes as her staff monitored the clients' whereabouts, forewarning her of their arrival. The first thing her patrons saw was a huge red ribbon across the front door. Leff invited them to cut the ribbon and enter for the first time. Inside, music was playing, candles were lit, and dinner was prepared. These moments of theater were typical of Leff, who thought this presentation enhanced the clients' delight upon seeing, for the first time, their dream fulfilled. Leff would be exhausted and excited in equal measure.

Leff was an active participant in the professional activities of the architecture and design community. In 1973, the year she graduated from Pratt, she lectured at the Architectural League of New York; the next year, she served on the League's Program Committee. Also with the League, Leff contributed to the Archive of Women in Architecture, which produced a traveling exhibit as well as the 1977 book *Women in American Architecture: A Historic and Contemporary Perspective*.

She also took seriously her position as a business owner, especially a woman business owner. Leff filled in the gaps left by her design training with a program established by the American Women's Economic Development Corporation, the first organization to provide entrepreneurial women

with management training and technical assistance. As Leff told *Interiors* magazine in 1981, "When it's your firm you've got to take care of everything: administration, personnel, insurance, taxes, marketing, contract negotiation, financial and long-range planning. When do I have time to design? These days it's after 5:30 and on weekends."

Leff maintained her affiliation with the Pratt Institute. She lectured on the relationship of social science and design. In 1990, she received the Distinguished Alumni Award and was invited to become a member of the school's board of trustees, where she served for ten years. The year 2000 signified the most important of her honors from Pratt, the prestigious Legends award. It was an important night for Naomi Leff, one she would remember with pride.

Through her relationship to the institution, Leff became acquainted with Pratt's president, Dr. Thomas Schutte. They were both active collectors of the decorative arts, often frequenting the same antiques shows. Leff would seek Schutte's judgment on an object's authenticity, origin, and value as she searched for clever acquisitions. The two also met for lunch two or three times annually at the University Club in Manhattan. Schutte said, "She was exasperated and frustrated with her master's not being a degree in architecture, *and* with the whole interior design and architecture curriculum. She found it belittling that architects

lord it over interior designers and, as always, wanted to find the root solution. In this case, it was to get a degree in architecture." But the demands of her career made it impossible to follow through.

Over several of their lunches, Leff and Schutte discussed the aging of Americans. Leff observed that current generations were living longer, and she considered the state of living for older people to be inadequate. She wanted to develop a new model for senior housing that would offer an aesthetic and architectural infrastructure responsive to the specific needs of the aging. Leff was always intrigued by the idea of extending her style to new building types and at the same time helping others in ways uniquely suited to her talents.

In 2004, Leff was completing the residence she considered her masterpiece, a twelve-thousand-square-foot penthouse apartment in Naples, Florida. Of the scheme, she said to her friend Barbara Ashley, "I'll never be able to do anything better than this." She was also more than ten years into the design of her own apartment—outside commissions always took precedence over her personal residence. She refused to allow her escalating health concerns to inconvenience her clients or interfere with her work and maintained an unrelenting work schedule, even giving directions from her hospital bed. She died from liver disease in New York on January 30, 2005. Naomi Leff & Associates was closed. Consummate teacher

and professional that she was, Leff bequeathed her archive to the Pratt Institute Library, and a majority of her estate was earmarked to establish a design scholarship in her name.

Leff was a unique talent with an informed vision that bridged invention and interpretation. She communicated the essence of design ideas, whether in a decorative molding, an item of furniture, a complete room. Her detailed compositions exuded restraint, understatement, and elegance. With extraordinary adaptability, the designer reveled in the diversity presented with each new commission. Dexterously combining historic styles with modern elements, Naomi Leff's works are a master class in what is achievable in a given space aesthetically, functionally, and practically. Purpose and determination, combined with a rigorous, discerning eye, drove her life entirely. Her contribution, and the individual works of art she created, will endure.

NOBODY SITS DOWN AND ARTICULATES A DREAM, BUT
OVER A PERIOD, FRAGMENTS OF THE DREAM BEGIN
TO APPEAR. MY DECISIONS INTERPRET IT AND BRING
IT INTO FOCUS. WHERE VISION COMES FROM IS NOT
IMPORTANT. WHAT MATTERS IS THAT WE ALL TAKE THE
STEPS FORWARD AT THE SAME TIME.

NAOMI LEFF

NAOMI LEFF & ASSOCIATES OFFICES
NEW YORK CITY » 1986

In 1986, Naomi Leff moved her company into an eighteenth-floor penthouse office on Twenty-seventh Street, where Naomi Leff & Associates would always remain. Her inspiration for the open loft space was the modernist, minimalist aesthetic of Le Corbusier. A floor of thirteen-inch-wide aged-pine planks was laid throughout the office. Black granite countertops stand out against white walls, and natural light floods in through the industrial skylight.

In the foyer, Leff designed saddle-leather seating to greet clients and colleagues alike. Also in the lobby are a model of a capital Leff designed for the Rhinelander Polo store and a pair of Frank Gehry Wiggle chairs, which were originally in her first office on Twenty-sixth Street. The Empire State Building dominates the view from the conference room and also from Leff's private office. The conference room, where she spent the majority of her time, was used for both design and presentation. Showcased in Leff's office were artifacts that were a source of particular pride or happiness, such as a mockup of a spindle from the staircase for the Polo store and a model of a Porsche similar to one she copiloted on a cross-country adventure.

THE RALPH LAUREN HOME COLLECTION
J. P. STEVENS & CO. SHOWROOM
NEW YORK CITY » 1982

Leff's concept for showcasing the Ralph Lauren Home Collection, based loosely on Bloomingdale's model rooms, was to create a series of realistic settings, each featuring a different look from the collection. The notion of presenting merchandise in a staged environment that reflected and romanced the products was to revolutionize retail.

Located within the J. P. Stevens skyscraper on the Avenue of the Americas, Leff's tableaus displayed and highlighted the Ralph Lauren merchandise so the buyers could see the items in context. She wanted each room, from a faithfully detailed yacht interior to a historically accurate log cabin, to be individual and full of substance. In fact, once Ralph Lauren saw Leff's log cabin design, he dispatched her to Colorado to work on the restoration of a ranch for his family.

According to Buffy Birrittella, Lauren's vice president of women's design and advertising, "The showrooms captured what Ralph Lauren wanted to say. It was an American lifestyle experience."

RHINELANDER MANSION
POLO RALPH LAUREN SHOP
NEW YORK CITY » 1986

Ralph Lauren envisioned his flagship store, set within the historic Rhinelander Mansion, as not only the most beautiful store in the world but also an environment of authenticity and integrity. It took three years for Leff to transform Lauren's vision into reality.

The building, on the corner of Madison Avenue and Seventy-second Street, was originally constructed between 1895 and 1898 as a grand family home for Mrs. Gertrude Rhinelander Waldo. The architects, Kimball & Thompson, loosely modeled the structure on a chateau in the Loire Valley. It is not known whether the building was ever finished to the original plans, and following its completion, the residence stood unoccupied for over twenty years.

For most of the twentieth century, the Rhinelander Mansion was occupied by antiques dealers and auction houses, with rental apartments on the upper floors. The ground floor was extensively modified at least twice, removing the bay windows and original entrance, while the second floor was altered and reconfigured. When Polo acquired the long-term lease for the five-story, twenty-nine-thousand-square-foot building, most interiors had been gutted and demolished, with the exception of the major ornamental spaces on the second and third floors.

Leff studied and retained every possible fragment of the original structure. She pored over books,

details, moldings, and materials, discovering and cloning elements. She restored the original entrance and installed new wood cabinetry and paneling that complemented the surviving ornamentation. A plan dating to the 1920s shows the configuration, but not the details, of a grand stair between the first and second floors; Leff used this documentary evidence to design a new formal stair. When the store was completed, most people had no idea that Naomi Leff had re-created the interiors from a demolished shell.

In a biography of Ralph Lauren, Colin McDowell wrote,

From its opening day, the Rhinelander captured the imagination of New York, the United States and the fashionable world. American broadcasting networks reported it as if it were the opening of a major museum or art institution . . . A year after its opening Women's Wear Daily, claiming the store to be one of Manhattan's hottest tourist attractions, said that between 1,000 and 15,000 customers went through its doors daily, shattering "expectations for its first year by doing in excess of $30 million, more than triple the pre-opening projection."

In a profile written in 1989, the *New York Times* reported, "Leff consulted the few original plans still existing, and, by digging into the bowels of the building, pieced together the rest. Upon removing the gigantic air conditioning units that had been

buried in the middle of the house, she uncovered the site of the original staircase. She then designed a grand mahogany stair that looks as though it has always been there. The ornamental plasterwork, which also appears to be original, was recast from surviving fragments." Three years later, *Times* architectural critic Paul Goldberger called the store "the most successful conversion of a New York house into a luxury emporium since Cartier took over the former Morton Plant residence on Fifth Avenue. It is . . . just the right balance between beautiful objects for sale and beautiful objects placed to enhance the experience of being in a stage set."

Ralph Lauren himself has said, "To me, it's the most beautiful store in the world: the details, the world it creates, the mix, the textures. It's a store that has an emotional impact. I've watched so many people come into it and be dazzled when they enter."

POLO RALPH LAUREN SHOP
BEVERLY HILLS, CALIFORNIA » 1987

For a store on Rodeo Drive in Beverly Hills, Leff proposed a more tropical interpretation of Ralph Lauren's aesthetic. Polo Beverly Hills was designed to capture the essence of the British colonial empire, the spirit of Kenya's Muthaiga Country Club, an old haunt of Karen Blixen and safari hunters.

Unlike previous stores for Lauren, Polo Beverly Hills was in a newly constructed building. Leff created a courtyard entrance filled with large planters and an abundance of tropical foliage that immediately transported customers to the luxurious lifestyle of an ealier era. This courtyard leads directly into the men's department. Leff had noted that men are hesitant about walking into a women's store, while women have no such reluctance, and allocated the space accordingly. A second entrance, complete with valet parking, on the other side of the building provides direct access to the womenswear.

Leff explained to journalist Colin McDowell in the *Guardian*, "Like all good clients, Ralph Lauren had a dream. He knew very well what he wished to achieve and it was my job to create the vocabulary to enable him to articulate that dream. That's my role."

SADDLERIDGE CONFERENCE CENTER
BEAVER CREEK, COLORADO » 1991

It was around 1990, when Leff received her Distinguished Alumni Award from Pratt, that she was approached by Shearson Lehman Brothers. On the basis of her work at the Rhinelander Polo store, the financial services company commissioned her to design and develop a conference center in Beaver Creek, Colorado. The firm envisaged an authentic Old West mountain lodge.

Leff assembled for SaddleRidge an extensive collection of Native American furnishings and artifacts that remains largely intact. For example, she acquired a set of Edward Curtis photographic negative plates from the early 1900s. With North American Indians as his subject, Curtis created an irreplaceable photographic and ethnographic record of more than eighty native nations. His portraits of Geronimo, Red Cloud, Chief Joseph, and Medicine Crow were included in the collection Leff obtained, and Curtis's photograph of Red Cloud takes pride of place above the fireplace in the center's main lodge.

Leff's affinity for Colorado and New Mexico is plain in all aspects of SaddleRidge. She purchased hand-woven Navajo rugs and striking Native American artifacts in auction houses and antiques shops alike. Among the distinguished objects are Annie Oakley's gun and memorabilia of William "Buffalo Bill" Cody. She obtained fine black-on-black

pottery by internationally sought-after artisans Maria and Julian Martinez. Their unusual technique contrasted ethnic and often geometric designs against the solid matte canvas of the pottery. This monochrome quality was especially appealing to Leff, who recognized a parallel in her own work.

Leff devised the vast chandeliers that hang from forty-foot ceilings in the main lodge. Lighting designer Craig Roberts, who collaborated with Leff on numerous projects, notes of the warm glow that appears to come from the chandeliers, "Naomi designed the most creative secondary canopy suspended from the ceiling—that is what actually created the glow; it wasn't the chandeliers as it appeared." The clients recalled that the finished interior was "exquisite, both warm and welcoming, but with a museumlike quality born of Naomi's attention to and creative interpretation of historical detail."

SaddleRidge was purchased by Vail Resorts in 1994, and Leff took up skiing so that she would have a reason to visit the lodge. She returned most often for Christmas holidays and long weekends with friends.

GIORGIO ARMANI BOUTIQUE
BOSTON, MASSACHUSETTS » 1992

Naomi Leff designed the Giorgio Armani boutique in Boston to reflect the subtle sophistication of the designer's aesthetic while at the same time introducing the look of his Milan salon to the United States. A grand axis, softened by curves and elegant materials, leads into the main entrance area, which is given over to accessories. Built-in ash display cabinets and paneling appear to float against the walls. This blond wood contrasts with the ebonized Brazilian cherry used for the other fixtures, fittings, and displays. Leff had enormous respect for the impeccable work of Luciano Cenacchi, the artisan who crafted Armani's shop fittings; she measured all other craftsmen against him.

The axial layout continues up the central stairs to the women's clothing, displayed near the back of the store. The second level echoes the material palette and the distinct chiaroscuro character of the first floor. Leff's room settings capture the essence of each product. Her expertise in visual presentation is manifested in the context and ambience of the store and its architectural form.

GIORGIO ARMANI BOUTIQUE
SAN FRANCISCO, CALIFORNIA » 1996

Giorgio Armani and Naomi Leff agreed that the designer's San Francisco store would break with the precedent set by his Milan flagship and the Boston boutique. Armani wanted an extremely modern, simple, and elegant, though intimate, space rather than a commercial environment. Leff's bold yet clean lines mirror the essence of Armani's clothing and accessory designs.

The existing building had intrusive structural columns throughout its interior space. Leff clad them in gypsum and made them an integral part of the design, using them to highlight the Armani dresses. Glass sheets flanking the central stair set off the columns. The black steel stair is softened with mahogany banisters. A soffit detaches the ceilings from the walls, providing a tranquil, floating sensation within the large space. This feel is reinforced by the display cases, shelving, and furniture groupings, which are set away from the walls.

Intimate seating areas with chairs, tables, and lamps balance Leff's use of metal, wood, glass, and leather. All screens, fixtures, and furniture are easily moveable so that the appearance of the store is ever-changing. Subtle colors harmonize with those in Armani's fashion designs; neutral tones in particular focus attention on the merchandise.

A/X ARMANI EXCHANGE
NEW YORK CITY » 1992

A/X Armani Exchange was a completely new venture for Giorgio Armani, a casual collection with an emphasis on denim. The development process was a long one in which the staffs of the Armani Corporation and Naomi Leff & Associates collaborated to define the business. Even the creation of the A/X logo would involve a think tank and an extended design process, independent of the store concept and development.

Leff had researched Armani and his company in depth, not only for A/X but for her previous work on his boutiques. For this project, she focused her attention on jeans. To Leff, denim symbolized relaxation, and her concept boards were built around merchandising jeans, traditionally work wear, as fashion apparel. The boards incorporated images of Armani's vacation home in Pantelleria as well as a little-known photograph of the designer wearing relaxed clothing and his signature enigmatic smile.

Once the concept was refined, Leff and Armani together chose the site in New York's Soho district. The design was inspired by Pierre Chareau's Maison de Verre—Armani's favorite piece of architecture—and incorporated details drawn from Quonset huts and the military post exchange, or PX. Industrial and practical materials worked with fixtures and displays to encourage self-sufficiency in shopping. Like those of a European open-air market, the store displays support independent browsing. In 1992, Leff won first prize from the Institute of Store Planners for A/X Armani Exchange. Her design set the precedent for hundreds of A/X stores worldwide, and she herself designed freestanding shops in New York, New Jersey, Florida, and California.

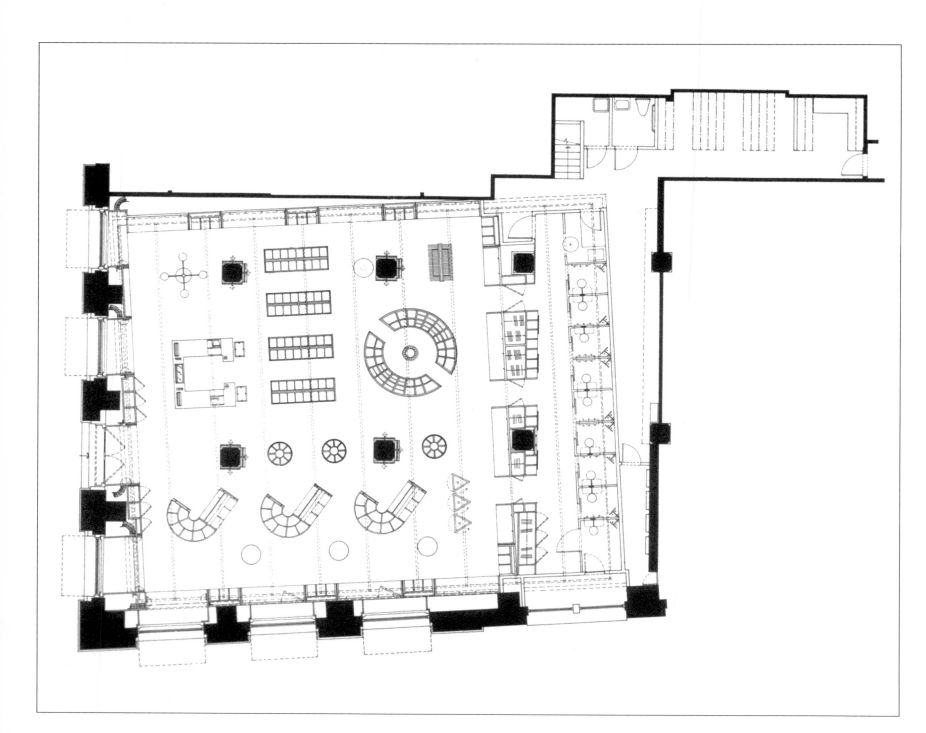

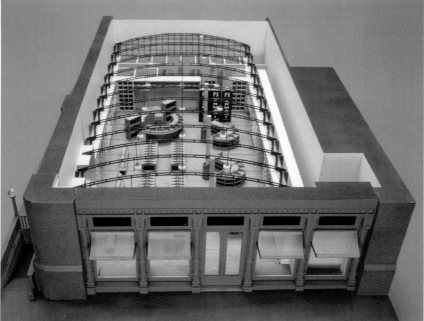

ARMANI JEANS / SIMINT

INSPIRATION OF PANTELLERIA
ISPIRAZIONI DI PANTELLERIA

ARMANI JEANS / SIMINT

DETAILS

WINDSOR BEACH CLUB
VERO BEACH, FLORIDA » 1994

Naomi Leff met Hilary and Galen Weston in the late 1980s when they commissioned her to design the hundred-thousand-square-foot Toronto flagship of their newly acquired Holt Renfrew stores in Canada. In 1989, the Westons founded Windsor, a resort of 416 acres on a lush barrier island in Florida between the Indian River and the Atlantic Ocean, eight miles north of Vero Beach. The seaside enclave is a tranquil and picturesque community.

The Westons asked Leff to design both their own cottage and the interiors of the Beach Club, the clubhouse at the heart of Windsor Beach. A social hub for the local residents, the eleven-thousand-square-foot Beach Club offers an elegant restaurant that overlooks a twenty-five-meter pool and private beach cabanas. On the ground floor is a drawing room and library with a billiards table; the dining room and a separate cocktail lounge are upstairs.

Leff's design evokes a British colonial retreat with Caribbean influences and complements the building's steeply pitched roof with open eaves and generously proportioned windows and doors. The drawing room has an elegant staircase and shuttered French doors that give onto the swimming pool. Cloche lanterns and white ceiling fans hang from white-painted beamed ceilings with inset tongue-and-groove paneling. The walls are painted in neutral tones, and the furniture is a tailored blend of traditional forms. Club chairs are upholstered in blue-and-white ticking or loosely covered in white burlap; sofas are covered in vibrant yellow-and-white floral patterns. Small rattan tables with wooden frames and larger, neoclassically influenced tables constructed from dark hardwoods are interspersed with the seating. Large terra-cotta pots filled with tropical plants accentuate the peaceful British colonial flavor.

DINING ROOM · VIEW EAST

HR HELENA RUBINSTEIN BEAUTY GALLERY & SPA
NEW YORK CITY » 2000

In 1998, the L'Oréal cosmetics company approached Leff to design the New York flagship for its range of new Helena Rubinstein cosmetics in the United States. Like many retail clients who worked with Leff, L'Oréal was looking to her to design a store that would define a brand. Leff's challenge for Helena Rubinstein was to combine a treatment salon intended to suggest privacy and pampering and a retail store meant to encourage traffic.

Leff helped L'Oréal select a large free-flowing space on Spring and Greene Streets in the Soho district of New York. The retail area on the ground floor featured a "makeup theater" for the latest Helena Rubinstein products along with a "vitamin C bar." Leff's always subtle lighting took on a heightened importance in the retail space. She and her lighting consultant spent hours perfecting a scheme that would allow customers an accurate, flattering view of makeup colors yet was bright enough to emphasize the subtleties of skin texture.

The lower floor accommodated the spa. Leff modeled a series of private rooms intended to evoke a deep sense of calm and well-being in the heart of New York City. The project played with light and silhouettes, and a feng shui expert was recruited to ensure that the layout conformed to the most benign forces of energy. The manicure and pedicure stations had a view of a peaceful inner garden. Translucent curtains let in the light but also offered privacy. Fabrics were selected to be crisp and spalike yet warm and cosseting. The individual rooms were minimal, with products and towels neatly tucked away in storage cabinets.

Margaret Sharkey, then general manager and later president of Helena Rubinstein USA, drove the project from the client side. Of Leff's work she said, "The spa was sublime. She approached her work as a piece of art, an expression of her creativity. It was her life."

94

1

2

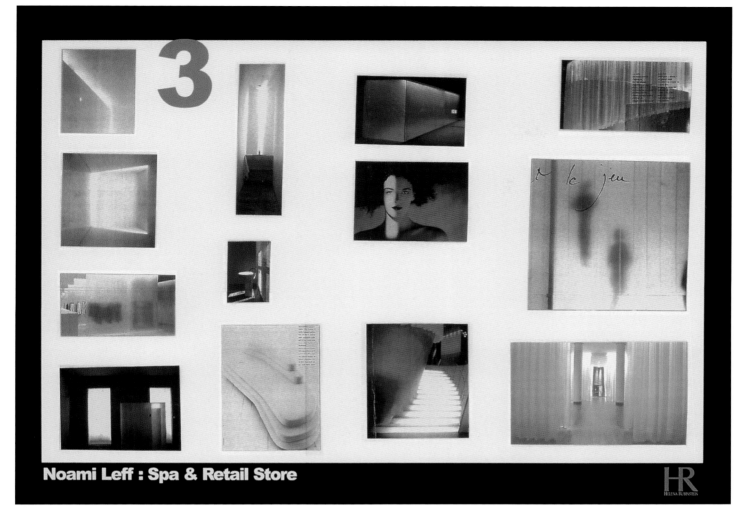

Noami Leff : Spa & Retail Store

Noami Leff : Spa & Retail Store

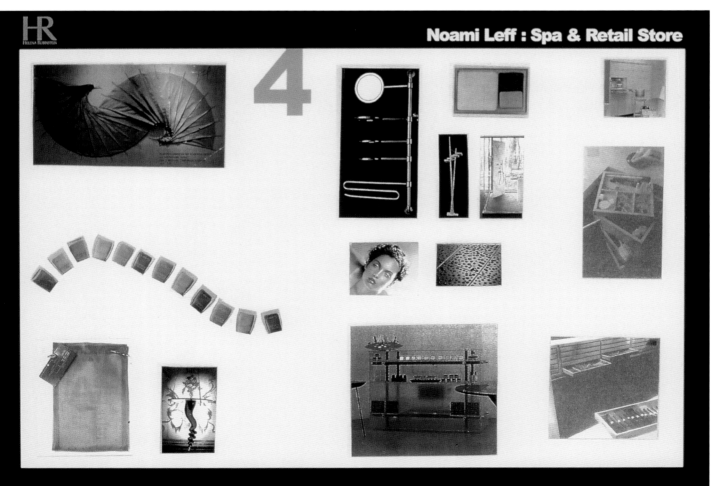

JERRY BRUCKHEIMER FILMS
SANTA MONICA, CALIFORNIA » 1996

Leff designed the offices for the Bruckheimer production studio as a balance between the modern and traditional techniques of the French Art Deco period. Materials included wooden beams, natural brick, glass paneling, polished plaster, and steel. Two-inch-thick black ebony shelving provided storage; custom brass light fixtures were fixed to the shelves. Putnam rolling ladders offered access to the higher shelves.

Jerry and Linda Bruckheimer, who worked with Leff on several projects, say, "We watched in awe as she effortlessly shifted from one gear to the next, conquering every facet of style, be it American Country or French Art Deco. She had a gift for adding those details that elevated good design to great, giving each project her inimitable 'Naomi touch.' She accomplished this with much flair and aplomb and her keen sense of humor." The Bruckheimers' offices were connected through a private side door. Linda Bruckheimer's desk was inspired by a piece by Paul Dupré-Lafon. The intricately designed secrétaire folds out to reveal a leather writing tablet and folds back so it can be locked.

Leff was meticulous about the scale of the furniture she designed for her projects. More often than not, she constructed a full-scale model of the piece, making alterations until she was satisfied. In this case, a pair of guest chairs in Linda Bruckheimer's office was submitted to this treatment.

Leff also designed Jerry Bruckheimer's desk, which has an oil-rubbed bronze base and a wooden top. It is long enough to host large meetings in his office. A separate seating arrangement consists of chairs and sofas upholstered in bold black velvets and leathers. A spiral staircase leads to a small seating area overlooking the production studio. The Bruckheimers recall, "Naomi's true genius was her ability to interpret her client's vision with minimal input. We came to our first meeting armed with a fistful of clippings and a stack of magazines. We leafed through book after book, pointing out one image or another. We realized a few weeks later that we could have saved our breath, for it was obvious that she had 'gotten it.' Not only did her concept hit the bull's eye, it reinvented it. Her genius continues to enrich our lives every day."

QUELLE FARM
EAST HAMPTON, NEW YORK » 1994

Filmmaker Steven Spielberg commissioned Leff to design the interiors for the cedar-shingled guest house of his family's East Hampton residence. Its volumetric exterior resembles a series of conjoined village buildings. Internally, a skylit gallery, proudly displaying the artwork of young visitors, ties the rooms together. Leff found this kind of project especially exciting. The guest house was designed by Charles Gwathmey, an architect for whom she had enormous regard, and the clients had a strong sense of design, notably a passion for the American Arts and Crafts period.

Leff dove into a study of the Arts and Crafts style from both a historical and a design perspective. She learned the individual styles of the masters of the period as well as the conceptual framework of design. Her original interior tempers a tasteful Arts and Crafts setting with occasional pieces of Art Deco, Vienna Secession, and American folk art—all design periods that share a simplicity and honesty of form. Random-width oak planks, tongue-and-groove cedar siding, and a brick fireplace maintain a continuity with the exterior.

When the project was completed, Steven Spielberg told *Architectural Digest,* "The best thing about Naomi's interior design is the selection of fabrics and their hues, even more than their textures." Leff herself commented, "Since Arts and Crafts furniture can be strong and powerful and the house is low and horizontal, I tried to keep the mood somewhat soft and romantic. I used muted colors to tie in all the different styles of art and furniture. I was also playing off the teal-blue trim of the architecture." And Gwathmey notes, "Naomi was able to reinforce the architectural integrity of a project through both counterpointal intervention and formal sensibility. Her fanatic attention to detail, craftsmanship, and installation realization infused her work with a density and quality that was unparalleled. Naomi Leff was a true collaborator."

HIRSCH RESIDENCE
WELLINGTON, FLORIDA » 1998

Neil Hirsch was introduced to Naomi Leff by the dealer who had, over many years, helped him establish his collection of American art. Hirsch asked Leff to create a period interior within his plantation-style home on the grounds of the Palm Beach Polo and Country Club. One special request was that Leff incorporate architectural elements from George Washington's Mount Vernon. The design of Washington's Potomac River estate is quintessentially American—open, welcoming, and democratic—and symbolizes the transition between the colonial era and the birth of the nation.

Leff's sparse yet immaculate backdrop for the client's collection of Queen Anne furniture and rare objects highlights the beauty and individuality of each piece. Her color palette was determined by the collection. Hirsch and Leff quickly established a rapport. The client recalls, "Naomi and I were on the very same wavelength. I would go to Christie's or Sotheby's the day before an auction to preview the hundreds—or *thousands*—of pieces and select four or five items. Without discussing it, Naomi would pick out the exact same four or five items."

A magnificent staircase, hand-carved to Leff's design, tested the woodworker's craft to the limit, especially the delicate curve atop the newel posts. Pieces from Hirsch's collection of Americana are judiciously positioned throughout the house. Notably, Leff placed a cigar-store Indian on wooden wheels and rolled it alongside the staircase. Antique chandeliers and sconces in the foyer and dining room were not electrified; they retain their original candlesticks. (The chandelier must be lowered to change the candles.) For practicality's sake, discreet downlighting was introduced. In the formal dining room, one of Gilbert Stuart's own replicas of his original "Athenaeum head" holds pride of place. The wood-paneled billiards room, with its wet bar and display of the client's polo awards, evokes the feeling of a gentleman's smoking parlor.

An authentic atmosphere was paramount to client and designer, even though the house was newly built. Hirsch's objective was a perfect restoration, not a pastiche or a reproduction. This is precisely the result Leff achieved, and the house remains today as it was when she completed it.

HIRSCH RESIDENCE
WATER MILL, NEW YORK » 2001

After Leff finished his residence in Wellington, Florida, Neil Hirsch commissioned her to update and upgrade his Federal Revival summer house, which sits on five acres in the Hamptons village of Water Mill backing onto Mecox Bay. Leff embellished and improved upon the existing period features to enhance the somewhat unexceptional house, transforming it into a subtle and authentic essay in historic detailing.

The designer left almost nothing untouched. She replaced the pine flooring throughout the house with dark-stained antique oak, enlarged the kitchen, and transformed Hirsch's office into a breakfast room with pine paneling, rush-seat dining chairs, and an oak dresser holding nineteenth-century Chinese porcelain. In the living area, she added crown molding and realigned the awkward paneling. Leff devised a new mahogany handrail for the wooden staircase in the entrance hall, and in the library she exchanged the original rough beams for more refined colonial ones. She renovated the baths and raised the ceiling in the master bedroom.

Leff's color palette was once again inspired by Hirsch's art collection, in this case American naive paintings from the 1850s. Subtle glazes on the walls and linen and damask materials emphasize the unique characteristics of the Queen Anne furniture.

In the dining room, Leff hung Thomas Skynner's 1846 portraits of Mr. and Mrs. Moses Pike. In the living area, she kept the windows clear and modern since window treatments were not needed for privacy. An antique Sultanabad rug on a large straw-colored handwoven carpet creates texture, and a molded copper Statue of Liberty weathervane of about 1890 on the mantelpiece lends an idiosyncratic note. In a guest bedroom, Leff supplemented Hirsch's pieces with a slant-front writing desk and a banister-back armchair. A Chippendale desk of about 1760 and a Sturtevant Hamblin painting, *Portrait of a Baby Holding a Rattle,* are in the master bedroom.

ASPEN LODGE
COLORADO » 1998

The spectacular location and views sold the client on this house, rather than any features of architecture or interior design. In fact, the client wanted to transform the interior into a vast, open space, retaining only the existing fireplace as required by local building regulations. To the client's initial vision of a modern loftlike interior Leff introduced and carefully integrated other influences. The finished house balances Art Deco principles and forms with design influences from Native American cultures.

Leff used a wide range of materials, from local fieldstone and butternut walnut to ebonized mahogany, wrought iron, and stainless steel. The color palette is drawn from the natural pigments in Native American rugs and from the surrounding views. A large picture window in the entry makes the most of the view of Aspen Mountain; the light fixtures are a bespoke design by Michael Adams, a skilled artisan with whom Leff worked on many projects.

The main living space is subtly divided into discrete parts. The more formal area combines geometrical decorative objects of the American West, sofas that Leff designed based on 1930s styles, and Josef Hoffmann chairs. An informal section, designed as a game room, contains a bar, three televisions, and a billiards table. The rugs in the living room, game room, and dining room are large-scale replicas of Navajo rugs Leff commissioned from weavers in Oaxaca, Mexico.

A sculptural red wall obscures the view to the bedroom wing. Leff was fixated on achieving a particular tone of red, an aesthetic element she considered an integral part of her design balance. The specialized artists of Concept Studio ultimately achieved the correct tone with a complex layering of pigments. Beyond the voluminous red wall, the master suite takes advantage of a 270-degree mountain view. Its private hallway, paneled in butternut walnut with jib doors, can either seal off the suite indistinguishably or present an open passage. In the master bathroom and dressing area, Leff designed a chair and mirror inspired by Paul Dupré-Lafon.

PENTHOUSE APARTMENT
NAPLES, FLORIDA » 2004

The owners of this extremely modern, twelve-thousand-square-foot penthouse apartment were, like so many of Leff's clients, return patrons. Along with a striking and unobstructed view of the junction between the Gulf of Mexico and the Atlantic Ocean, the project presented Leff with a series of difficult challenges. The apartment is situated on the top floor of an oval concrete tower, with two centrally located elevator shafts interrupting the internal volume. Leff was determined to create order and symmetry while making full use of the flow created by the gently curving walls.

The color palette was informed by the natural tones of the surrounding landscape: the wide span of sea and sky, the dramatic view of the setting sun. Inspired by the almost transparent nature of the architecture, Leff attempted to transcend any sense of barrier between exterior and interior spaces. She used bold shapes in the architecture and finishes, as well as in the furniture, fabrics, and lighting, to unite the arching exterior features with practical, rectilinear internal spaces.

On the walls is Venetian stucco; on the floors, large slabs of polished Bardiglio Imperiale marble. Leff turned the lack of a traditional datum point for the square tiles into an advantage: laid on the diagonal, they offset the curved shape of the building. The lighting design proved to be Leff's most imaginative collaboration with her longtime lighting consultant, Craig Roberts. Inspired by the Chinese principle of yin and yang—the importance and strength of two opposing forces—the scheme begins in the entry with bars of light on the ceiling that match strips of black marble in the floor. In the living area, concealed lighting emanates from the soffits, and bubblelike casts of light are created by circular pinspots above the seating areas.

Between the entrance columns are two gull-wing walls clad in ornately grained Tamo ash. In the niche created by one of these walls is a bar, its alabaster countertop lit from within. The tulip chairs in the bar, precisely carved to Leff's design, contrast with the circular seating arrangements in the living area, which are elegantly upholstered in purple and white. Boulders on the stone floor inside the living room create a sense of continuity between indoor and outdoor spaces.

A corridor leading to the guest suite and game room passes between the lounge on one side and the media room on the other. The lounge is delineated by a low cabinet topped with an abacus-inspired screen; all elements of this piece, including the junction with the ceiling, reflect a profile of waves. A Leff-designed saltwater fish tank is the focal point of the lounge area. The media room, a spectacular red-lacquered "space within a space," is set apart by sliding doors featuring a central oculus. Made of glass and rice paper, the oculus is adorned with an Oriental metal screen. For the interior of the media room, Leff chose a chocolate brown color with accents of a specific red, which is also used in other rooms of the apartment. On the walls are gold saris. Leff commissioned a painting on a black-lacquer screen, based on an original by Jean Dunand, into which she worked a portrait of the clients' own fair-haired pooch.

LAPPIN RESIDENCE
NEW YORK CITY » 1992

Built in 1851, the Upper East Side building that was to become Joan Lappin's home was occupied by the Salvation Army for nearly a century. In 1977, when Lappin bought the property, it contained seven apartments. Her aim was to restore it to its former grandeur and create a family residence within. Her research found it had never been a splendid building, so it was necessary to create an entirely new architectural persona.

Lappin turned to Naomi Leff to transform the building. The client identified Rockefeller Center and the interior of her boat as favorite places, leading Leff to conceive a design with strong Art Deco references. The vessel in particular was inspiring, because yacht design is especially known for clever ways of maximizing space. Leff pored over photographs of the grand ocean liners of the Art Deco era, such as the *Normandie*.

Leff developed from her studies a luxurious composition with a vertical emphasis. A staircase runs through all four floors as a singular element, visually reinforcing the feeling of being aboard a yacht. An elliptical wood column alludes to a mast; the balustrade—two steel strips, encasing a series of steel circles, appearing to float on top of a paneled base—represents a yacht's capping rail. Construction of the stair was especially complex.

Leff paneled the rooms on the parlor floor in a honey-toned, flat-cut anigre. Each panel conceals a closet, keeping the rooms neat and free of clutter. Lappin and Leff took multiple trips to Paris to buy the antique furniture and accessories. The stained-glass windows in the master bathroom are Leff's homage to Frank Lloyd Wright.

PARK AVENUE RESIDENCE
NEW YORK CITY » 2002

The clients for this large apartment commissioned Leff based on *Architectural Digest*'s feature on the Aspen lodge. They were impressed by her ability to harmoniously combine apparently disparate elements. Leff, in turn, was delighted by their collection of distinguished Art Deco pieces. Clients and designer evidently shared a similar sense of design; in fact, the clients called their collaboration with Leff "a master class in Art Deco."

The introduction to the apartment is a semicircular foyer that provides a view to the living areas beyond. A pair of French iron gates from the 1930s defines the entry to the dining room; Leff extended the gates in order to fit the high ceilings. Beyond the doorway is a 1930s rosewood dining table designed by Maxime Old.

In the drawing room, a Jean Dunand painting hangs above a wrought-iron demilune Art Deco console signed by Paul Kiss. Two armchairs by Alfred Porteneuve, covered in chocolate-brown suede, sit next to a coffee table with a cracked eggshell top and a Leff-designed fluted base. On the coffee table are a set of three Linossier

vases—Leff collected such vases herself—and a Dunand bowl. For the floor, Leff selected a late-nineteenth-century Kirman carpet.

A stepped ceiling profile housing a central lighting soffit unites the drawing room with a study beyond. The two rooms are divided by a pair of Edward Grant doors featuring signs of the zodiac. The study, intended for use by the gentleman of the house, is decidedly masculine. A sofa occupies a niche behind a Giacometti coffee table. Leff arranged a coin collection at the forefront of the bookshelves in rows of adroitly designed shallow slots. The clients were particularly keen to incorporate subtle decorative details, and Leff addressed this request specifically.

A corridor off the entrance hall leads to the private quarters. An office for the lady of the house contains an ebony table of about 1925 with intricate ivory inlay details and an ebony armchair with a leather-upholstered seat. The dressing room has glass doors etched with a stylized tulip design inspired by René Lalique. Leff designed the sycamore paneling and full-height cabinetry in the

style of Jean-Michel Frank. Generous mirrors alternate with raised paneling on the wardrobe doors. A central column integrates low cabinetry and a demilune stool.

In the master bedroom is a Leff-designed wardrobe with inset panels of shagreen in a nuanced light blue-green. The seating arrangement includes an occasional chair by Jules Leleu, a table by Jacques Quinet, and a signed Daum Nancy lamp. Leff installed two ovoid Barovier lamps beside the bed and suspended a René Lalique chandelier above. A central ceiling coffer with gently curved corners and a high reveal at the windows conceal curtain mechanics and ducting.

FORBES RESIDENCE
NEW YORK CITY » 2004

With their primary residence in Michigan, Sidney and Madeline Forbes were in the habit of using the St. Regis Hotel as their New York base. When the couple decided to establish a permanent pied-à-terre, one tailored to their own design inclinations, they commissioned Leff, having been taken with one of her boutiques for Giorgio Armani. The Forbeses, well versed in art and design, urged Leff to create something slightly more traditional while maintaining some modern aspects. The 2,500-square-foot gem, located within a fifty-one-story glass tower in the center of Manhattan, combines pieces from the late nineteenth century with Art Deco from the 1920s and 1930s.

To marry the various components of the design, Leff resolved to create a consistent backdrop. For the main living areas, she chose a honey-toned pear wood for the paneling, with main fields framed by a simple flat beading. Where the lower and upper panels meet, two beads join to form a dado. This feature, deliberately placed quite low, serves to thrust the ceilings higher, maximizing the sense of space. The dado is also functional, separating the storage spaces concealed behind the wooden panels. Leff's finely calibrated lighting makes the warm wood appear to glow from within. On the floors throughout the living spaces she laid French sandstone.

The entry is dominated by a Henry Salem Hubbell painting hanging above a French wrought-iron console. In the dining area are a Biedermeier table and chairs, hewn from auburn fruitwoods. A niche within the wood paneling shelters Abbott Fuller Graves's *Afternoon at the Pond*. The sitting room has floor-to-ceiling windows at one end, enhancing a view over the famous skyscrapers of midtown Manhattan. Hidden behind two paneled doors with backlit, figurative, René Lalique glass inserts is a bar, and facing back into the room is a pair of antique wood-framed chairs upholstered in fine hand-woven chenille.

Leff upholstered the walls of the master suite in silk; a wool carpet shares the same golden tone. Wide ribs of fabric soften the wall behind the Leff-designed bed. Pear-wood paneling and a built-in vanity unit provide storage in the dressing room. The curtains throughout the apartment hang plumb straight; the headers and ends are tucked neatly into the window reveals.

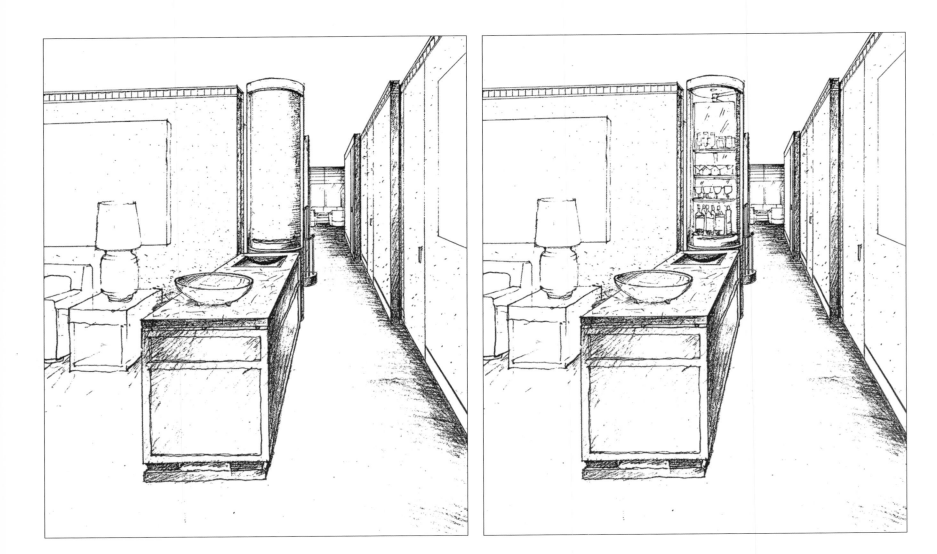

NAOMI LEFF APARTMENT
NEW YORK CITY » 1993–2005

In 1993, Naomi Leff bought an apartment in a chic Manhattan building at Seventy-fifth Street and Madison Avenue, across from the Whitney Museum. From the day she acquired the apartment until the day she died twelve years later, at least one member of her staff was assigned the task of committing her plans to paper. Invariably, more pressing work got in the way, and the staff member was reassigned to the task that took priority. At the time of her death, Leff had plans, elevations, and perspective sketches, as well as furniture and artwork purchased in Paris, London, and New York. Sadly, she never occupied the apartment.

Leff fell in love with this particular apartment because of the proportions of the rooms and the ceiling heights. The configuration of the apartment made creating a beautiful dining room a particular challenge, and Leff gave the space countless hours of consideration. She created an internal bow on the window wall with built-in soffits to house a tidy curtain stack. An eight-seat dining table is hinged in the middle to follow the curve of this wall; the inventive table also pivots into a straight position for more conventional dining. Sliding doors opposite the bow separate the dining room from the kitchen. Leff loved food, both preparing it and serving it to her guests, so in the kitchen she designed a large center island that extends into the dining room as a bar. Shaped to encourage free passage, the island provides ample storage space as well as a surface for food preparation and an area for informal gathering.

In contrast to the asymmetrical arrangement of the kitchen and dining room, the living area has a strong axis centered on the fireplace wall. The room is poised between a generously proportioned corridor—practically the width of the room itself—and vast double-height windows directly opposite. Bifold partition doors give access to the dining room and are mirrored by a pair concealing a recessed bar. The four corners of the room are gently curved, and a soffit in the ceiling echoes the floor plan. Concealed lighting in the soffit provides warm illumination.

Leff conceived an elegant library to house her voluminous collection of books; she planned it to double as a guest room. An entrance hall just before the library leads to her master suite. The double entry doors hinge outward and tuck away to reveal two substantial dressing rooms; for the bath, she devised a sail-shaped vanity. The floor plan reflects many of Leff's signature features. There is no doubt that this apartment would have become a spectacular showcase for the best of her design brilliance.

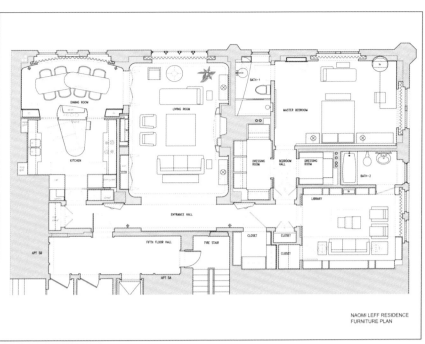

NAOMI LEFF RESIDENCE
FURNITURE PLAN

Project List

RETAIL

Anne Klein Store
» Minneapolis, Minnesota;
Manhasset, New York
Client: Anne Klein and
Company

The Arcade, The Market,
Citicorp Center
» New York, New York
with Judith Stockman &
Associates
Client: Citibank

A/X Armani Exchange
» Costa Mesa, California;
La Jolla, California; Santa
Monica, California; West
Hollywood, California;
Miami, Florida; Somerset
Mall, Troy, Michigan; Short
Hills Mall, Short Hills, New
Jersey; New York, New York
Client: Simint USA

Emporio Armani
» Boston, Massachusetts
Client: Giorgio Armani
Corporation

Emporio Armani
» Toronto, Ontario, Canada
Client: Holt Renfrew & Co, Ltd.

FAO Schwarz
» Stamford, Connecticut;
New York, New York
Client: FAO Schwarz, Co.

Giorgio Armani Boutique
» San Francisco, California;
Palm Beach, Florida;
Boston, Massachusetts
Client: Giorgio Armani
Corporation

Giorgio Armani Boutique
» Chicago, Illinois
Client: A.R. Boutique

Gucci
» San Diego, California;
Las Vegas, Nevada
Client: Gucci America, Inc.

Helena Rubinstein Beauté
» New York, New York
Client: Helena Rubinstein
Foundation

Noelle Beauty Spa
» Atlanta, Georgia;
Great Neck, New York
Client: The Gillette Company

Polo Ralph Lauren,
Rhinelander Mansion
» New York, New York
Client: Polo Ralph Lauren
Corporation

Polo Ralph Lauren
» Beverly Hills, California
Client: Jerry Magnin
Company

Polo Ralph Lauren
» Greenwich, Connecticut
Client: Polo Greenwich Group

Polo Ralph Lauren
» Birmingham, Michigan
Client: Claymore Shop

Polo Ralph Lauren
» Manhasset, New York
Client: Perkins Shearer

Polo Ralph Lauren
» Philadelphia, Pennsylvania
Client: Richard I. Rubin Co, Inc.

Polo Ralph Lauren
» Montreal, Quebec,
Canada; Deauville, France;
Paris, France; Munich,
Germany
Client: Louis Dreyfus
Company

Polo Ralph Lauren
» Tokyo, Japan
Client: Seibu Corporation
of America

The Robert Floyd Store
» Palm Desert, California
Client: Fitz and Floyd, Inc.

Salvatore Ferragamo
» Beverly Hills, California;
San Francisco, California;
Vancouver, British Columbia,
Canada
Client: Ferragamo
Finanziaria S.p.A.

Wilkes Bashford Women
» San Francisco, California
Client: Wilkes Bashford
Company

SPECIALTY RETAIL

Anne Klein Boutique
» Bloomingdale's, New York,
New York; Saks Fifth Avenue,
New York, New York
Client: Anne Klein and
Company

A/X Armani Exchange
» Bergdorf Goodman;
Bloomingdale's; Macy's;
Neiman Marcus; Saks
Fifth Avenue
Client: Simint USA

Giorgio Armani
» Bergdorf Goodman; Bloom-
ingdale's; I. Magnin; Neiman
Marcus; Saks Fifth Avenue
Client: Giorgio Armani
Corporation

Giorgio Armani
Le Collezioni for Men
» Bergdorf Goodman, New
York, New York; Saks Fifth
Avenue, New York, New York
Client: Giorgio Armani
Corporation

Holt Renfrew
» Calgary, Alberta, Canada;
Vancouver, British Columbia,
Canada; Toronto, Ontario,
Canada; Montreal, Quebec,
Canada
Client: Holt Renfrew & Co, Ltd.

Saks Fifth Avenue
Beauty Salon
» New York, New York
Client: Regis Corporation

SFA Real Clothes Boutique,
Saks Fifth Avenue
» San Francisco, California;
Chevy Chase, Maryland;
Boston, Massachusetts;
Minneapolis, Minnesota;
New York, New York
Client: Saks Fifth Avenue

SFA The Works Boutique,
Saks Fifth Avenue
» Denver, Colorado;
Chicago, Illinois; New York,
New York
Client: Saks Fifth Avenue

Wynn Las Vegas:
Bags, Belts & Baubles;
Brioni Men's & Women's
Wear; The Gallery and
The Gallery Shop; Wynn
LVNV & Chocolat
» Las Vegas, Nevada
Client: Wynn Design
Development

RETAIL PROTOTYPES

A/X Armani Exchange
In-Store Shops
» New York, New York
Client: Simint USA

Carolyn Roehm
» Japan
Client: Carolyn Roehm

Christian Dior
» Paris, France
Client: Christian Dior

Giorgio Armani
In-Store Shops
» Milan Italy
Client: Giorgio Armani
Corporation

Giorgio Armani Collezioni
In-Store Shops
» New York, New York
Client: GFT/Giorgio Armani

Gucci Stores
» Milan Italy
Client: Guccio Gucci

HR Helena Rubinstein
Beauty Gallery and Spa
» New York, New York
Client: HR Helena Rubinstein

Polo Ralph Lauren
In-Store Shops
Client: Polo Ralph Lauren
Corporation

Promenade at A&S
» New York, New York
Client: A&S/Federated
Department Stores

Saks Fifth Avenue
Private Label Boutiques
» New York, New York
Client: Saks Fifth Avenue

SHOWROOMS

A/X Armani Exchange
» New York, New York
Client: Simint USA

Fila Sports USA
» New York, New York
Client: Fila Sports USA, Inc.

Project List *continued*

The Ralph Lauren Home
Collection / J. P. Stevens
& Co. Showroom
» New York, New York
*Client: Polo Ralph Lauren
Corporation*

Two's Company
» New York, New York
Client: Two's Company, Inc.

OFFICES
Belvedere Farm
» Sunning Hill, Berkshire,
England
Client: W. Galen Weston

Burlington Northern
Railroad Corporate Offices
» Washington, D.C.
*Client: Burlington Northern
Railroad*

Dreamworks
» Los Angeles, California
*Clients: Steven Spielberg,
David Geffen, and Jeffrey
Katzenberg*

Giorgio Armani
Corporate Offices
» New York, New York
*Client: Giorgio Armani
Corporation*

Gramercy Capital
Corporate Offices
» New York, New York
*Client: Gramercy
Capital Management
Corporation*

Jerry Bruckheimer Films
» Santa Monica, California;
Disney Studios, Burbank,
California
Client: Jerry Bruckheimer

Naomi Leff & Associates
» New York, New York
Client: Naomi Leff

Universal Studios
» Los Angeles, California
Client: Ron Meyer

USA Networks, Inc.
» New York, New York
Client: Barry Diller

DEVELOPMENT PROJECTS
Ardleigh Court
Residential Renovation
» Montclair, New Jersey
Client: Milton Ehrlich, Inc.

Bridgewater at Belair
Public Spaces
» Clearwater, Florida
*Client: York Trillium
Development Corporation*

300 Bloor Street East
Public Spaces
» Toronto, Ontario, Canada
*with Ricardo Bofill Taller de
Arquitectura
Client: York Trillium
Development Corporation*

Store and Restaurant
» Kamakura, Japan
Client: Daiichi Showa Co., Ltd.

HOSPITALITY
Chinatown Dim Sum
» Cedarhurst, New York

Emporio Armani Express
» Boston, Massachusetts
*Client: Giorgio Armani
Corporation*

Lindsay Gray's Restaurant
» New York, New York

Minskoff Cultural Center
» New York, New York
Client: Park East Synagogue

SaddleRidge
Conference Center
» Beaver Creek, Colorado
*Client: Shearson Lehman
Hutton, Inc.*

Swenson's Ice Cream
Store, Bloomingdale's
» New York, New York

Windsor Beach Club,
Windsor Golf Club Brasserie,
Windsor Inn
» Vero Beach, Florida
*Client: W. Galen and Hilary
Weston*

RESIDENCES
Bleckman Residence
» New York
*Clients: Neil and Cookie
Bleckman*

Conyers Farm
» New York
*Clients: Ron and Cheryl
Howard*

Cruise Residence
» California; Colorado;
Sydney

Motor Yacht *Alibi*
» Sydney
*Clients: Tom Cruise and
Nicole Kidman*

Diller Residence
» California
Sailing Yacht *Mikado*
» Georgia
Client: Barry Diller

Forbes Residence
» New York
*Clients: Sidney and
Madeline Forbes*

Geffen Residence I + II
» New York
Geffen Residence
» Florida
Client: David Geffen

Grey Residence
» California
Clients: Brad and Jill Grey

Hirsch Residence
» Florida; New York
Client: Neil Hirsch

Katzenberg Residence
» California; Utah
*Clients: Jeffrey and Marilyn
Katzenberg*

Lampert Residence
» Colorado; Connecticut
Client: Edward Lampert

Lappin Residence
» New York
Client: Joan Lappin

Double RL Ranch
» Colorado
Lauren Residence
» New York
*Clients: Ralph and Ricky
Lauren*

Leff Residence
» New York
Client: Naomi Leff

LeFrak Residence
» New York
*Clients: Richard and Karen
LeFrak*

Meckler Residence
» New York
*Clients: Alan and Ellen
Meckler*

Nespola Residence
» New York
*Clients: Richard and Faye
Nespola*

Sherman Residence
» Florida; New York
*Clients: Bruce and Cynthia
Sherman*

Spielberg Residence I + II
» California
Quelle Farm,
Spielberg Residence
» New York
*Clients: Steven Spielberg
and Kate Capshaw*

Tisch Residence
» California
*Clients: Steve and Jamie
Tisch*

Weinstein Residence
» Connecticut
*Clients: Harvey and
Eve Weinstein*

Windsor Beach Cottage
» Florida
*Clients: W. Galen and
Hilary Weston*

Wolk Residence
» New York
*Clients: Elliot and Nancy
Wolk*

AIRCRAFT
Gulfstream III,
Gulfstream IV
*Clients: Tom Cruise and
Nicole Kidman*

Gulfstream IV
*Clients: Jerry and Linda
Bruckheimer*

Gulfstream IV
*Client: Shearson Lehman
Hutton, Inc.*

RAILROAD CARS
Missouri River Business Car,
Lake Superior Dining Car
*Client: Burlington Northern
Railroad*

Acknowledgments

In August 2005, six months after Naomi Leff died, I started working as one of a team of designers on what is currently the largest sailing yacht in the world. Several years earlier, as an interior designer with Naomi Leff & Associates, I had contributed to a yacht project for the same client. Immediately, Naomi, and all that I had learned under her tutelage, came to mind. Very specific thoughts of her work inspired me, and I wished there was a pictorial book of her most influential projects for me and everyone else who esteemed her work. Thus was born the concept for this book.

I would first like to thank Naomi's dear friend and executor of her estate, Barbara Ashley, for encouraging me to produce a preliminary proposal; her acceptance of this document granted me full access to the Pratt Institute Library and the wealth of Leff's archive, which she had bequeathed to Pratt. Barbara also shared with me Naomi's treasured artifacts, business papers, and personal effects and even combed the storage facility with me. And she spent countless hours with me on the telephone—both of us in various parts of the world—reviewing and commenting on my manuscript.

My thanks to Gianfranco Monacelli for agreeing to publish this book, to editorial director Andrea Monfried for gently guiding me through to the end, to expert production director Elizabeth White for her clear-sighted input, to marketing director Nicolas Rojas, to assistant editor Stacee Lawrence, and to graphic designer Michelle Leong for developing the pure layouts I believe Leff would have appreciated.

Lorraine Smith, visual resources curator of the Pratt Institute Libraries, reliably and efficiently provided me and The Monacelli Press with images from Leff's archive.

I am grateful to Paige Rense, editor in chief of *Architectural Digest*, for sharing some memorable moments and conversations she had with Naomi over the years, for giving her considered opinion on Naomi's talent and sophistication, *and* for accepting my invitation to write the foreword. Margaret Dunne, executive editor of *AD*, followed up scrupulously.

Pamela Krausmann recollected for me details vital to Naomi's concept work. She and I were holed up together in a Manhattan storage facility as we searched for valuable research materials among Leff's effects, and she aided me in the selection of images from Leff's archive at Pratt.

Thanks to Carol Sullivan, who once managed Naomi Leff & Associates, for joining me in sifting through yet another storage facility, this one in New Jersey. We gathered a substantial amount of materials from Leff's files, and it was a real adventure, one that I won't forget.

Many thanks to former Naomi Leff associates Eva Frank, Mark Janson, and Frank Visconti, who took the time to meet with me, providing critical information regarding projects completed as long as twenty years ago. Charles Baran, former vice president and managing director of NL&A, and Denise Kuriger, head of interiors at NL&A between 1996 and 2000, offered remembrances of projects. I am grateful to NL&A architects David Griffin, Stephen Lomicka, Joel Harper, Marina Lanina, Carmen Malvar, and Ramon Malvar, who supplied drawings and information, and to NL&A interior designers Wendy Konradi, Tanya Sim, Mary Foley, Nina Nielsen-Norwood, and Peggy Gubelmann, who contributed to my understanding of the work.

Thanks to the clients who took the time to meet me, in person or on the telephone, to share specifics about Leff's process: Neil Hirsch, Margaret Sharkey, Karen Cohen, Buffy Birrittella, Joan Lappin, Bruce and Cynthia Sherman, and Francine Kittredge. Jerry and Linda Bruckheimer were kind enough to offer their thoughts of Naomi in this book. And I am grateful that Naomi's clients have permitted me to use images of their projects in this publication.

Thanks to Charles Gwathmey, who wrote about collaborating with Naomi. Bill Ehrlich, a long-term friend and kindred spirit of Naomi's, gave me insight into the nature and quality of her character. Dr. Thomas Schutte, president of the Pratt Institute, was precise in his analysis of the academic aspect of Naomi Leff.

Craig Roberts, Naomi's lighting designer of twenty years, described to me her work from his perspective, and author and former editor of *Interior Design* magazine Stanley Abercrombie provided me with swift and pertinent data.

Thanks to photographer David Churchill, who traveled with me to Florida to photograph the penthouse Naomi considered her masterpiece, and to the clients, who generously made it happen. Keith Collins from Frederick Fisher and Partners provided images from Jerry Bruckheimer Films.

I am grateful to my father-in-law, John Isaac, a retired British lawyer and lecturer in legal studies with over thirty years experience heading the largest interior design practice in Wales. He is currently writing a biography on Grand Duke Dimitri Pavlovitch of Russia, and he set aside his project to help me investigate the vast Ralph Lauren archive and then to refine my manuscript.

Last, I express my utmost thanks to my husband and fellow designer, Alexander Isaac. He really should be the coauthor, since he helped me with every aspect of this demanding project for more than a year and a half. He has, whether he wanted to or not, become somewhat of an expert on the complicated woman who was Naomi Leff, interior designer.

Photography Credits

Numbers refer to page numbers.